EXTREME SURVIVAL IN THE MILITARY

SURVIVAL AT SEA

EXTREME SURVIVAL IN THE MILITARY

EXTREME SURVIVAL
IN THE MILITARY

SURVIVAL AT SEA

CHRIS McNAB

Introduction by Colonel John T. Carney. Jr., USAF-Ret.
President, Special Operations Warrior Foundation

MASON CREST

Mason Crest
450 Parkway Drive, Suite D
Broomall, PA 19008
www.masoncrest.com

Printed and bound in the United States of America

10 9 8 7 6 5 4 3 2 1

Series ISBN: 978-1-4222-3081-7
ISBN: 978-1-4222-3084-8
ebook ISBN: 978-1-4222-8776-7

Cataloging-in-Publication Data on file with the Library of Congress.

Picture Credits
Corbis: 16, 20, 23, 34, 43, 46, 50, 54, 56, 58, 59, 63, 65, 74 ; **TRH**: 6, 11, 21, 24, 32, 33, 84, 86, 88; **/US Army**: 36; **/US Dept. of Defense**: 8, 17, 18, 39, 40, 44, 77, 78, 82; **/US Navy**: 12, 13, 14, 28, 30, 70
Illustrations courtesy of Amber Books, De Agostini UK and the following supplied by Patrick Mulrey: 79

ACKNOWLEDGMENT
For authenticating this book, the Publishers would like to thank the Public Affairs Offices of the U.S. Special Operations Command, MacDill AFB, FL.; Army Special Operations Command, Fort Bragg, N.C.; Navy Special Warfare Command, Coronado, CA.; and the Air Force Special Operations Command, Hurlbert Field, FL.

IMPORTANT NOTICE
The survival techniques and information described in this publication are for educational use only. The publisher is not responsible for any direct, indirect, incidental or consequential damages as a result of the uses or misuses of the techniques and information within.

DEDICATION
This book is dedicated to those who perished in the terrorist attacks of September 11, 2001, and to the Special Forces soldiers who continually serve to defend freedom.

CONTENTS

KEY ICONS TO LOOK FOR:

 Text-Dependent Questions: These questions send the reader back to the text for more careful attention to the evidence presented there.

 Words to Understand: These words with their easy-to-understand definitions will increase the reader's understanding of the text, while building vocabulary skills.

 Series Glossary of Key Terms: This back-of-the book glossary contains terminology used throughout this series. Words found here increase the reader's ability to read and comprehend higher-level books and articles in this field.

 Research Projects: Readers are pointed toward areas of further inquiry connected to each chapter. Suggestions are provided for projects that encourage deeper research and analysis.

 Sidebars: This boxed material within the main text allows readers to build knowledge, gain insights, explore possibilities, and broaden their perspectives by weaving together additional information to provide realistic and holistic perspectives.

INTRODUCTION

Elite forces are the tip of Freedom's spear. These small, special units are universally the first to engage, whether on reconnaissance missions into denied territory for larger, conventional forces or in direct action, surgical operations, preemptive strikes, retaliatory action, and hostage rescues. They lead the way in today's war on terrorism, the war on drugs, the war on transnational unrest, and in humanitarian operations as well as nation building. When large scale warfare erupts, they offer theater commanders a wide variety of unique, unconventional options.

Most such units are regionally oriented, acclimated to the culture and conversant in the languages of the areas where they operate. Since they deploy to those areas regularly, often for combined training exercises with indigenous forces, these elite units also serve as peacetime "global scouts" and "diplomacy multipliers," a beacon of hope for the democratic aspirations of oppressed peoples all over the globe.

Elite forces are truly "quiet professionals": their actions speak louder than words. They are self-motivated, self-confident, versatile, seasoned, mature individuals who rely on teamwork more than daring-do. Unfortunately, theirs is dangerous work. Since "Desert One"—the 1980 attempt to rescue hostages from the U.S. embassy in Tehran, for instance—American special operations forces have suffered casualties in real world operations at close to fifteen times the rate of U.S. conventional forces. By the very nature of the challenges which face special operations forces, training for these elite units has proven even more hazardous.

Thus it's with special pride that I join you in saluting the brave men and women who volunteer to serve in and support these magnificent units and who face such difficult challenges ahead.

Colonel John T. Carney, Jr., USAF-Ret.
President, Special Operations Warrior Foundation

SEAL commandos rush ashore with their breathing apparatus. SEALs training is so tough that the drop-out rate is over 65 percent.

WORDS TO UNDERSTAND

maritime: Having to do with the sea.

indicators: Signs of something.

precede: Go before.

SEAS, OCEANS, AND WEATHER

The sea shows no mercy when it comes to survival; your first mistake in a maritime emergency is likely to be your last. You must master every ocean survival technique in order to live in this unforgiving environment.

Around 71 percent of the Earth's surface is covered by water. It is therefore vital that you learn how to survive in this environment. In particular, finding drinking water and food are serious problems for the survivor at sea, though the other dangers that the sea poses to the survivor should not be underestimated. The SEALs (U.S. Navy Sea, Air, and Land Teams) know how to cope with them all.

First, the SEAL gets to know the environment he or she faces. The temperature of surface water in the ocean can range from 100°F (38°C) in tropical regions to 28.4°F (–2 °C), the freezing point of seawater, in polar regions. The average temperature of the ocean surface waters is around 62.6°F (17°C).

But the conditions of the sea vary enormously with the weather. Around the poles in winter, there are violent storms characterized by snow, winds of up to 40 miles per hour (64 km/h), and temperatures as low as –122°F (–50°C). Storms in the Atlantic and Pacific oceans can result in waves higher than a three-storied house. In contrast, in some areas of the Atlantic, Pacific, and Indian oceans, there are times and places where there are no surface winds at all. The sea in these conditions becomes incredibly still, with no wind to help you travel if your boat does not have a motor.

Although the ocean is cold and unforgiving, SEALs must be prepared to jump in from a helicopter, such as this Boeing CH-47 Chinook.

Even the strongest swimmers are in danger from ocean currents. SEALs are trained to recognize, and adapt to, the four main types of current: tidal, wind, littoral, and rip.

Waterspouts (the equivalent of tornadoes at sea) are common off the Atlantic and Gulf coasts and along the coasts of China and Japan. Hurricanes and typhoons occur in the warm areas of all oceans during the summer and fall. They can last for up to two weeks.

Sailors and SEAL soldiers are very aware of signs that indicate which way the weather is likely to turn. Two good **indicators** are the wind and the clouds. By recognizing the direction and changes of wind, the types of cloud, and the likely weather they indicate, you can prepare better for either good or bad weather. In the summer, in particular, the land is warmer than the sea during the day, but it is colder than the sea at night.

Clouds can be incredibly useful for surviving at sea because they can tell you a lot about what type of weather is heading your way. (See the diagram on the next page.) There are four main groups of clouds, categorized on the basis of height above the Earth: cirrus, cumulus, nimbus, and stratus. The first type is cirrus cloud. These occur around 20,000 feet (6,096m) above the Earth. Cirrus clouds are composed of ice particles. They are feathery and long, and appear as streaky bands. They are known as mare's tails. These clouds can often indicate fine weather, but when they are accompanied by a regular north wind in cold climates, they sometimes **precede** a blizzard. Within cirrus comes cirrostratus and cirrocumulus. Cirrostratus consists of a fine veil of whitish clouds, darker than cirrus. When cirrostratus follows cirrus across the sky, bad weather may be about to arrive, so now is the time to make preparations. Cirrocumulus clouds give a different message. These clouds are small white balls arranged in groups, and they indicate good weather.

Next come cumulus clouds. Fluffy, white, and heaped together, these clouds are often indicators of fine weather. They can appear around midday on a sunny day. If they pile up and push higher into the atmosphere, they can become storm clouds. In the third category, nimbus clouds paint the whole sky in a uniform gray color. This can mean bad weather, but it is even more serious if you see cumulonimbus. Towering into the atmosphere, these clouds are dark with flat bases and rounded tops. Sometimes they form an anvil shape at the top, looking like cirrus. They often mean sudden heavy showers of rain, snow, or hail. If a thunderstorm occurs, you can expect a strong wind from the direction of the storm as well as a rapid drop in temperature.

The final category is stratus. These are low clouds composed of water droplets that make up an even, gray layer of cloud. They inevitably mean rain or snow. Within stratus is altostratus. Holes in this layer mean that the weather may not be too bad. Finally comes nimbostratus. These rain-bearing clouds have a low base and consist of thick layers.

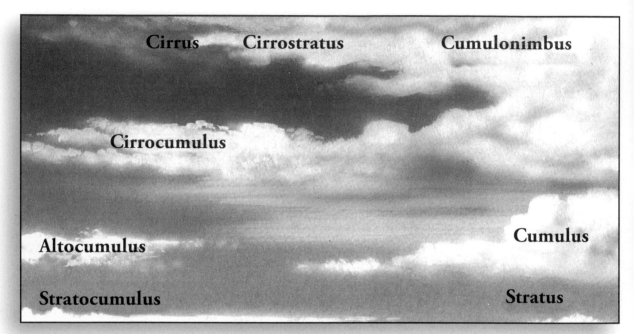

Recognizing the various cloud formations can indicate what type of weather is approaching, and the type of kit required for an operation.

The clouds can tell you what the weather will be like, but you also need to be able to read the winds. A good way of doing this is using what is known as the Beaufort Scale. This scale helps you read how much danger you are in.

THE BEAUFORT SCALE

Description & wind speed (knots)	Land signs and sea signs
0 Calm (less than 1)	Smoke rises. Sea surface smooth.
1 Light air (1-3)	Smoke drifts, wind vanes are still.
2 Light breeze (4-6)	Wind felt on face. Vanes move. Rustling leaves.

3 Gentle breeze (7-10)	Light flags extended. Leaves in motion. Large wavelets. Crests begin to break.
4 Moderate breeze (11-16)	Small branches moving. Dust raised. Small waves (1-4 ft) with numerous whitecaps.
5 Fresh breeze (17-21)	Small trees sway. Moderate waves (4-8 ft) with many whitecaps and some spray.
6 Strong breeze (22-27)	Large branches in motion. Whistling wires.
7 Near gale (28-33)	Trees in motion. Walkers buffeted. Seas piling up. Foam (waves are 13-19 ft).
8 Gale (34-40)	Twigs broken off trees. Difficult to walk.
9 Strong gale (41-47)	Slight structural damage. Shingles may blow away. High waves (23-32 ft) with dense foam.
10 Storm (48-55)	Trees broken or uprooted. Considerable structural damage. Very high and heavy rolling waves (29-41 ft).
11 Violent Storm (56-63)	Exceptionally high waves (37-52 ft). Foam patches cover the sea.
12 Hurricane (64+)	Air filled with foam. Waves over 45 ft, with the sea completely white with driving spray.

MAKE CONNECTIONS:
THE WORLD'S OCEANS AND SEAS

The following chart lists the sizes of the world's oceans and seas in square miles. The Pacific Ocean is by far the biggest at almost 64 million square miles.

	Square miles	Square km
Arctic Ocean	5,427,000	14,056,000
Atlantic Ocean	41,100,000	106,400,000
Baltic Sea	163,000	422,200
Bering Sea	884,900	2,291,900
Caribbean Sea	1,049,500	2,718,200
East China Sea	482,300	1,249,200
Gulf of Mexico	615,000	1,592,800
Hudson Bay	475,800	1,232,300
Indian Ocean	28,350,000	73,556,000
Mediterranean Sea	1,144,800	2,965,800
North Sea	222,100	575,200
Pacific Ocean	63,800,000	165,250,000
Red Sea	169,100	438,000
Sea of Japan	389,100	1,007,800
Sea of Okhotsk	613,800	1,589,700
South China Sea	895,400	2,319,000
South China Sea	895,000	2,318,000
Yellow Sea	156,000	404,000

TEXT-DEPENDENT QUESTIONS

1. How much of the Earth's surface is covered by water?

2. Using the Beaufort Scale, explain how you can tell if a hurricane is on its way.

3. Which oceans are the second and third largest?

As soon as the wind reaches numbers 5 or 6 on this scale, you should head for safety if you are in a small boat at sea. The SEALs always need to know what weather is heading their way for their missions. But sometimes even they accept that disaster may strike.

RESEARCH PROJECT

Find out more about clouds and what kind of weather they can indicate by researching them online or at the library. Draw or print from the Internet a picture of each type of cloud. Explain next to each image how that kind of cloud is formed and what it can indicate in terms of weather.

WORDS TO UNDERSTAND

retain: Keep, hold on to.

submerging: Putting under water.

priorities: Things that are most important.

elements: Weather conditions.

dinghy: A small, open boat.

prevailing winds: The winds coming from the most common
direction in a particular place or season.

proximity: Nearness.

vegetation: Plants.

SWIMMING AND SURVIVAL

Being thrown into the sea can literally take your breath away. The SEALs teach you that in these situations there is no substitute for a clear and calm mind that helps you work out how to survive.

In survival circumstances, SEALs teach that it is better to **retain** clothing when in the water. If abandoning a ship or aircraft, take whatever warm clothing is available as well as easily portable food (chocolate and candies). Do not jump into the water with an inflated life jacket, because the impact may be dangerous.

Once in the water, inflate your life jacket, swim steadily, and look for any floating objects, such as pieces of wood, that will help you to keep afloat. Use a life raft if there is one around.

If you are escaping from a downed aircraft, swim or paddle upwind, especially if the plane is on fire. Remember, any large object, such as a plane or boat, will create suction when it sinks beneath the surface and can drag survivors down with it. Therefore, get away from the plane or boat as soon as possible.

If there is burning oil on the water, attempt to swim under it, using an underwater breaststroke. (You may need to deflate or throw away your life jacket for this.) When you need to come up for air, leave enough time to clear a space in the burning area by pushing the water aside from beneath the surface. Then take in enough breath and, if possible, look to check the shortest route to clear water before **submerging** again, straight downward, feet first.

Before putting on their face masks, SEAL divers spit into the mask, then wash it out. This stops the mask fogging up in the water.

Swimming in the ocean for long periods is extremely tiring, especially if the water is cold. Floating on your back can provide much needed rest and ensure your head stays clear of the water.

Once clear of immediate danger, practice relaxing by floating on your back with your face above the water. This will let you gather your energy before swimming again to the nearest life raft or large floating object. If no life raft is available, but you are wearing a life jacket, get in the Heat Escape Lessening Posture (HELP) to keep as much body warmth as possible. The principle of HELP is keeping the head clear of the water, since a lot of heat is lost through the head and neck.

If you have nothing to help you stay afloat, you can save energy by relaxing into a crouching position, which will let your body float just below the surface of the water, and then move your arms to bring your head up to the surface to breathe before relaxing into the crouch position again. However, these measures are only temporary—you must get out of the water. If you do not, you could quickly freeze to death.

If you are lucky, you might have found your way into a life raft. When in a raft, the SEALs' immediate **priorities** are rescue, protection from the **elements**, and water to drink. Obey the following rules: Give first aid to any wounded survivors. Check that any signaling equipment is ready to use. This may include flares, emergency radio, and flags. Save batteries of signaling equipment by using them only when search aircraft or ships are in range. Salvage any useful material that may be floating nearby. (It can be tied to the **dinghy** to provide more space inside.) Ensure that one member of the crew is attached to the life raft with a line, in case it tips over and is blown away. If you have supplies of drinking water, do not drink it all at once—ration it out. Check available supplies of food.

Follow the survival instructions you find on the life raft. Remove wet clothing when you can, and dry it out. In a cold climate, huddle together to share warmth. In a hot climate, keep at least one layer of clothing on to protect the body from the direct powerful light and heat of the sun. If any survivors have dry clothes, they should share them with those who are wet. Those who are wet should be given the most sheltered positions in the raft, and they should be allowed to warm their hands and feet against those who are dry. If possible, give extra water rations to those suffering from cold exposure. You should exercise fingers, toes, legs, arms, shoulders, and buttocks to help keep you fit and strong. In a sitting position, put your hands under your armpits and raise your feet slightly off the ground. Keep them up for a minute or two. Try to exercise at least twice a day.

These actions should help you survive. But your goal is to be seen or to find safety. Your chances of being found are greatest if you are close to the area where rescuers were last in radio contact. Stay in the area for at least 72 hours to give them a chance to find you. The following actions will help your chances of being rescued. Put out a sea anchor in order to stay close to the site. When open,

In emergencies, the Heat Escape Lessening Position (HELP) retains body heat, although, ideally, a wet suit or dry suit should be worn.

MAKE CONNECTIONS: ABANDONING SHIP

Abandoning ship is a frightening experience, but you must act quickly. Follow these SEAL guidelines and save your life.

- Put on warm, preferably woolen, clothing, including a hat and gloves. Wrap a towel around your neck.
- Take a flashlight.
- Grab chocolates and hard candies if possible.
- Do not inflate your life jacket until you leave the ship.
- When jumping overboard, first throw something (anything wooden) that floats and jump close to it.
- Air trapped in clothing will help buoyancy; do not take off your clothes in the water.

the anchor will help to keep the raft in one place. When closed, it will cause the life raft to be pulled along by the current. Signaling and navigation equipment should be carefully protected from the elements, but have them ready to use quickly.

Exercise leadership skills where necessary and give people tasks to do (such as signaler, navigator, spotter, and fisherman). Try to find out who has any specialized skills that might be useful. If you are not the leader, concentrate on carrying out your particular job effectively as best you can. Do not interfere with other people's tasks unless asked. You will be thinking most clearly in the early stages of survival when you are reasonably well fed and watered, so make plans then that you can remember and follow if things become difficult and you become weaker. Put up any permanent signals, such as a flag. Keep a log,

MAKE CONNECTIONS: SWIMMING STROKES FOR SURVIVORS

- **Dog paddle:** good stroke for when you are clothed or wearing a life jacket.
- **Breast stroke:** good stroke for swimming underwater or in rough seas.
- **Side stroke:** a useful stroke to let one arm have a rest.
- **Back stroke:** gives the arm and chest muscles some relaxation. It is also less tiring because it is easier to float in this position.

recording the **prevailing winds**, weather, currents, and state of the crew on board. This will help in such matters as navigation.

If rescue has not come or if, for any reason, you consider this to be unlikely (it may be that no one knows you are there), then the SEALs say that you should try to find land. There are several signs that may tell you that land is nearby. A stationary cumulus cloud can mean an island nearby. Birds will often be heading toward land in the afternoon and evening. Look out for the particular types of birds and the direction in which they are flying. If it is the morning, they will most likely be heading away from land. A lagoon can create a greenish reflection on the underside of clouds. Floating vegetation and pieces of timber may indicate the **proximity** of land. Water that is muddy with silt has probably come from the mouth of a large river that is nearby. Deep water is dark green or dark blue; a lighter color indicates shallow water and perhaps land.

Once you have sighted land, your goal is to reach it as soon as possible. If you are swimming, wear your shoes and at least one thickness of clothing. Use

TEXT-DEPENDENT QUESTIONS

1. If you are escaping from a sinking boat or plane, why is it important to get away from the plane or boat as soon as possible?

2. What does HELP stand for in this chapter and when should you use this?

3. If you are in a survival situation, why should you make a plan as soon as possible rather than waiting?

4. What are six signs that might mean that land is nearby?

5. Describe the best technique for swimming ashore.

side or breast stroke to save your strength. Water is calmer in the sheltered side of a heavy growth of seaweed. Do not swim through it; crawl over the top by grasping the **vegetation**. Swimming ashore can be difficult because of sea currents and hidden rocks. Yet the SEALs know the right techniques. Ride in on the back of a small wave by swimming forward with it. In high waves, swim toward the shore in the trough between waves. Put your face down and submerge yourself beneath the waves, then swim forward in the next trough. If caught beneath a large wave, let it pass over and then push off the bottom with your feet, or swim to the surface if in deep water. When landing on a rocky shore, aim for the place where the waves rush up onto the rocks, not where they explode with a high white spray. To land, advance behind a large wave into the breakers. Face the shore with your feet in front, two to three feet (60–90 cm) lower than your head. In this way, your feet will absorb shocks when you land or hit submerged rocks or reefs, and you will not get injured.

RESEARCH PROJECT

There are many books that tell true stories about survival at sea. Read one and then write a report about what happened to the people in the story. Did they use any of the techniques for survival described in this chapter? Here are some books to look for in your library:

Adrift: Seventy-Six Days Lost at Sea by **Steven Callahan**

Fatal Forecast: An Incredible True Tale of Disaster and Survival at Sea by **Michael J. Tougias**

Overboard! A True Blue-water Odyssey of Disaster and Survival by **Michael J. Tougias**

Alone: Orphaned on the Ocean by **Richard Logan** and **Tere Duperrault Fassbender**

If your library doesn't have any of these books, ask your librarian to help you find another true survival-at-sea story—or ask if she can order one of these books for you.

If you do not reach shore behind the wave you have selected, swim using your hands only. Get in a sitting position as the next wave approaches and carries you to shore. Once ashore, you will need other survival skills. But whether you are on land or at sea, in order to survive you need to know where you are going.

WORDS TO UNDERSTAND

reliable: Something you can count on or trust.

axis: A straight line connecting two points.

illuminated: Lit.

hostile: Unfriendly.

NAVIGATION AND SIGNALING

Seas can be incredibly easy to get lost in. There are no landmarks as there are on the dry land, so you need to know how to find out which direction you are heading in at all times.

If you are in a properly equipped life raft, it should contain navigation equipment with instructions. If you do not have the usual equipment, there are several methods of navigation. The sun can often help you calculate where you are heading. The sun rises in the east and sets in the west. Between sunrise and sunset, you can get a rough estimate of direction by using your watch. Aim the hour hand at the sun. The point halfway between the hour hand and twelve o'clock will show the approximate direction of true south if you are in the northern hemisphere, and the approximate direction of true north if you are in the southern hemisphere.

The night stars are a **reliable** guide and have been used by navigators for thousands of years. The most important star for navigation in the northern hemisphere is Polaris (North Star), which stands over the North Pole. Polaris can be identified in the sky by following a line through the two brightest stars of the constellation known as Ursa Major (Great Bear), or the Big Dipper. In the southern hemisphere, a constellation known as the Southern Cross is used as a guide. The four brightest stars form a cross tilting to the side. Follow the **axis** of the two furthest apart and continue an imaginary line five times

A U.S. Navy officer plots a course on a naval chart. He uses a pair of dividers and a magnifying lens, and records his actions in a logbook.

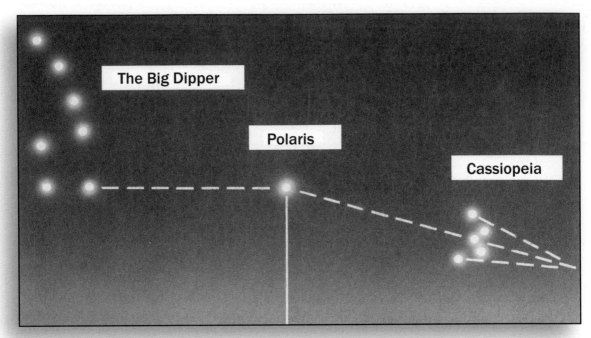

If navigating without a map by night, Polaris, or the North Star, and the Big Dipper, are the best guides for finding the direction of north.

the length of this axis. At about the point where this imaginary line ends, you will find south.

Star movement can be used to determine your position. Watch a star over two fixed points for 15 minutes. You will see it move. In the northern hemisphere, the following rules apply: If the star is rising, you will be facing east. If the star is falling, you will be facing west. If the star is looping to the right, you will be facing south. If the star is looping to the left, you will be facing north. Reverse these rules if you are in the southern hemisphere. The moon can also give you some direction information. If the moon rises before the sun sets, the **illuminated** side will be on the west. However, if it rises after the sun sets, the illuminated side will be on the east.

When SEALs are at sea, they often carry a large range of signaling equipment

MAKE CONNECTIONS: INTERNATIONAL RESCUE CODES

SOS

Pyrotechnics: Red flare.

Auditory signal: 3 short, 3 long, 3 short—repeat every minute.

Light flashes: 3 short, 3 long, 3 short—repeat every minute.

HELP NEEDED

Pyrotechnics: Red flare.

Auditory signal: 6 blasts in quick succession—repeat every minute.

Light flashes: 6 flashes in quick succession—repeat every minute.

MESSAGE UNDERSTOOD

Pyrotechnics: Red flare.

Auditory signal: 3 blasts in quick succession—repeat every minute.

Light flashes: 3 flashes in quick succession—repeat every minute.

with them to attract attention to themselves. If you have them, use flares and dye markers (which spread brightly colored dye in the sea), to attract the attention of a ship or aircraft. If you do not have any signaling equipment, attract attention to yourself by waving clothing and other materials, which

TEXT-DEPENDENT QUESTIONS

1. Describe how to locate the North Star in the night sky.
2. List 5 ways you could get rescuers' attention.
3. What does it mean if an airplane flashes green lights as it passes over you?

should be brightly colored if possible. Sea markers should only be used in daylight. (They normally last for around three hours.) A mirror or reflective surface can be used for long-range signaling.

All flares should be handled carefully. Keep them dry and secure, and when firing, point them upward and away from yourself and anyone else in the raft. Use them only when you are sure that they will be seen. A shiny, reflective surface is also an excellent way of attracting attention to yourself. On a sunny day, mirrors, polished canteen cups, belt buckles, or other objects will reflect the sun's rays. Always practice signaling before you need it. Mirror signals can be seen for 62 miles (100 km) under normal conditions and over 100 miles (160 km) in a clear environment. There are several other ways in which you can attract attention to yourself. Many life jackets are fitted with a whistle. Blow the whistle hard to alert boats to your presence. Flashlights or strobe lights can also be seen over great distances.

If aircraft pass overhead, use bold waving actions to attract the crew's attention. Hold a cloth in each hand to make your signals even clearer. Whenever you

RESEARCH PROJECT

People have used the stars to keep from getting lost for thousands of years. Sometimes this kind of navigation is called celestial navigation. Use the Internet or the library to find out more about its history. Who were some of the ancient groups of people who used the stars to navigate? Why is this kind of navigation still used in modern times? Tell your class what you discover.

are making signals, always do so with clear, large movements. (Remember you will be a great distance from the aircraft.) An aircraft that has understood your message will tilt its wings up and down in daylight or make green flashes with its signal lights. If pilots have not understood your message, they will circle their aircraft during daylight or make red flashes with their signal lights at night. Once pilots have received and understood your first message, you can send other messages. Be patient; do not confuse the person flying the aircraft. Since the ocean is so huge, you might not be found for some days. Survival is going to be tough, but the SEALs are trained to find food and drinking water even in this **hostile** outdoor environment.

WORDS TO UNDERSTAND

securing: Holding down, fastening.

essential: Absolutely necessary.

improvising: Making something using whatever is

handy.

FINDING FOOD AND WATER

You are surrounded by water at sea—unfortunately, none of it is drinkable. You must find ways to provide yourself with food and drinking water or you might not survive for more than a few days.

At sea, water is your most precious commodity, as any Navy SEAL will tell you. Do not be tempted to use sea water for drinking or for mixing with fresh water. It is likely to cause vomiting and serious illness. The minimum requirement of fresh drinking water is one pint (475 ml) a day. Follow these water ration rules strictly to increase your chances of survival.

Day 1: Give no water. The body can make use of its own water reserves. Be strict with this rule.

Days 2-4: Give 14 fluid ounces (400 ml) if available.

Day 5 onward: Give two to eight fluid ounces (55–225 ml) daily, depending on water availability and climate.

If you have no way of measuring the fluid, just come up with a ration that will give you all a supply of water for over a week, and do not drink for the first 24 hours, or until you have a headache. A big problem is that you lose your body's

A SEAL is surrounded by water when at sea, but it is not drinkable. In high temperatures, up to three gallons (13.6 liters) is required per day.

water through sweating. Follow these SEAL guidelines strictly for reducing your use of body water. In hot climates, reduce sweating by staying still and saving your energy. Brush dried salt off the body with a dry cloth. Try to sleep and rest as much as possible. Try not to get seasick. Vomiting causes you to lose valuable fluids. Relax and focus your mind on other tasks. Suck on a button to make saliva and reduce your desire to drink. In a hot climate, keep out of direct sunlight and dampen clothes during the day to keep cool, but do not get too wet or get water in the raft. If there is not enough water, do not eat, because the food will absorb water from your body. In a hot climate, in particular, food is secondary to water. Watch out for rain and make sure you catch it in a tarpaulin and/or other containers. Store as much as possible and always sip water in a slow, steady way to avoid vomiting. Let the body absorb the water rather than overfilling your stomach. Moisten your lips and mouth before swallowing.

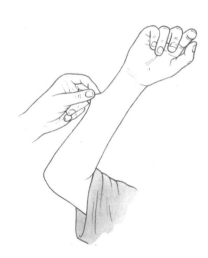

Dehydration is one of the biggest killers at sea. To test if someone is dehydrated, pinch the skin and let go. If it goes back slowly, then the person is probably dehydrated and needs urgent medical attention.

Apart from the rain, there are other ways of finding water. One is a solar still. A life raft may be supplied with a solar still. Read the instructions carefully because the still will not work unless the sea is relatively calm. You can also make a solar still by placing a plastic sheet over a container and **securing** it with whatever is on hand. Place coins or a stone in the center of the sheet. In the morning, the sun raises the overall temperature of the air to produce vapor. Water then condenses on the underside of the sheet and runs down into the container.

Icebergs provide a source of water in cold climates. Old sea ice will have lost much of its saltiness, but new ice will taste unpleasant. Old ice can be recognized by its smooth shapes and blue color. Do not approach large or moving icebergs, since these may crush the life raft or overturn it suddenly.

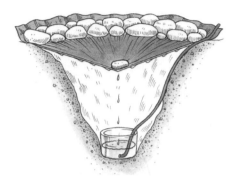

A solar still is a useful method of getting water from the air itself, and can be made at sea if you have the right equipment.

It is advisable to eat nothing for as long as possible and remember not to eat too much if little water is available. However, food will be **essential** if you are to survive for a few days. When it comes to finding food, fish are the obvious choice for SEALs. Fish will be your main food source. Flying fish may even jump into your raft! In the open sea, without land in sight, fish are generally safe to eat. However, do not eat fish that are brightly colored, covered with bristles or spines, or those which puff up or have parrotlike mouths or teeth like humans. Also, avoid fish eggs in clusters or clumps; these will be poisonous. Catching fish is not easy if you are **improvising**. Yet the SEALs are expert fishermen as well as expert soldiers. Follow their advice for safe fishing.

Do not touch the fishing line with your bare hands when reeling in, and never wrap it around your hands or tie it to an inflatable dinghy. The salt on it makes a sharp cutting edge that is a danger to your hands and the raft. If you have gloves, wear them when handling fish; that way, you will not get fins or fish teeth in your skin. Pass a net under your raft from one end to the other—fish and turtles are attracted to the shade under your raft. (You need at

MAKE CONNECTIONS: LIFE RAFT CONTENTS

Soldiers stranded at sea will stand a much better chance of finding food, not to mention being rescued if they have access to a professional life raft. Contents you might find in a life raft include the following:

Sea anchor	Paddles
First-aid kit	Fishing line
Bellows	Survival leaflets
Bailer	Repair kit
Flares	Knife
Sponge	Fresh water
Eating equipment	Can opener
Seasickness pills	Flashlight

least two people to perform this.) Use a flashlight to attract fish at night. Make improvised hooks from small pieces of wire and small bright objects.

Use the guts of a fish, or organ meats, that you have caught previously or a small fish as bait to catch larger fish (though they can also be used as food). Cut loose any fish that are too large to handle and do not fish if sharks may be near. Head for large shoals of fish, but remember that sharks and barracuda may also be present. Be careful not to puncture the dinghy with the fish hooks. You can also bind a knife to an oar to use as a spear to catch fish.

The process of gutting and preparing fresh fish or shellfish can be done swiftly and cleanly with a sharp knife.

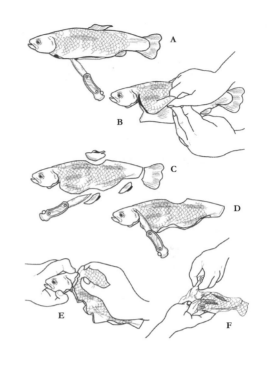

Experiment with different ways of fishing and find out what works best for you. Once you have caught a fish, you should gut it immediately. (See the diagram on page 35.) This is not pleasant, but it has to be done. Slit the fish with your knife from the anus to just behind the gills (A) and pull out the internal organs (B). Clean the flesh, then cut off the fins and tail (C). Cut down to, but not through, the spine. Cut around the spine, finishing behind the gills on both sides (D). Insert your thumb along the top of the spine and begin to pull it away from the flesh (E). The ribs should come out cleanly with the spine (F). Eat the fish raw.

The SEALs will also show you that fish are not all that you can eat at sea. All seabirds are edible, for example. They will be attracted to your raft as a perching place. Wait until they land on your raft, then try to grab them before they fly away. However, the best method is to use a hook covered in fish, which can be trailed behind the boat. The hook gets stuck in seabirds' throats. Use a noose or net, similarly camouflaged, to trap their legs.

Some seaweeds can also be eaten. They should be eaten only if they are firm to the touch and odorless. Do not eat slender, branched varieties of seaweed. These contain acids that will make you feel ill. Make sure that there are no sea

TEXT-DEPENDENT QUESTIONS

1. If you're stranded at sea, how much water should you drink on the first day?
2. How do you make a solar still?
3. What sorts of fish should you avoid eating?
4. List three guidelines to keep in mind when eating seaweed.
5. What is plankton?

creatures attached to the seaweed before eating it. You can collect seaweed around shorelines and in mid-ocean. Remember that seaweed absorbs fluids when your body is digesting it, so it should not be eaten when water is scarce. You should eat only small amounts of seaweed at a time, because it can cause you to have bowel movements or need to urinate, losing more precious water from your body.

If fish, birds, and seaweed are not enough for survival, then a SEAL will also eat plankton. Plankton consists of tiny plants and animals that drift around or swim weakly in the oceans. They can be caught by dragging a net through the water. Plankton contains many nutrients, yet it can make you ill when eaten in large quantities. If you are living solely on plankton, therefore, you must eat small quantities at first. In addition, you should ensure you have an adequate supply of drinking water; digesting plankton will use up your body fluids. Each plankton catch should be thoroughly checked before you eat it: remove all jellyfish tentacles (be careful not to get stung), discard the plankton that have

RESEARCH PROJECT

Find out more about plankton online and in the library.

Why are these tiny creatures so important to life in the ocean? What sea animals depend on them for life? Here is a list of different groups of plankton:

- zooflagellates

- diatoms

- phaeophyta

- siphonophores

- ciliates

- dinoflagellates

- corepods

- krill

For each group of plankton, draw a picture illustrating an example. Then write how each group moves and eats. Make a note of one more interesting fact about each group.

become jelly-like, and check for species that are spiny. If the catch contains large amounts of spiny plankton, you can dry or crush it before eating.

As you can see, it is possible to live off the sea even when you are miles away from land. However, the sea is also a cruel place to be. The SEALs will now teach you what dangers to avoid.

WORDS TO UNDERSTAND

lethal: Deadly.

scavengers: Animals that feed on dead plants and animals, as well as human garbage.

aggressive: Ready or likely to attack and become violent.

potentially: Possibly.

tropical: Having to do with the area of the world near to the equator.

subtropical: Having to do with the area of the world that lies between the tropics and the temperate zone.

temperate: Not too hot and not too cold. The area of the world known as the temperate zone is where North America is.

fatalities: Deaths.

adrenaline: A chemical released into your body when you are excited or afraid, which gives you greater strength.

reef: A ridge of rock, sand, or coral just beneath the surface of the waves, which is dangerous to boats.

duct: Tube.

DANGERS

The sea is home to some of the world's most dangerous creatures, including sharks, lethal poisonous fish, and massive killer whales. Knowing how to avoid these animals can save your life.

The first dangerous sea creature most people think of is a shark. Sharks are **scavengers** and live in almost all seas and oceans. They feed more actively at night, and especially at dawn and dusk. After dark, they move toward the surface and into shallow waters. They are attracted to garbage, body wastes, and blood, and also by weak splashing movements similar to those of a wounded fish. A shark cannot stop suddenly or turn quickly in a tight circle, and it will rarely jump out of the water to take food. For this reason, people on rafts are safe unless they dangle their legs or arms in the water.

The main types of shark that have been known to attack humans are listed below, but be aware that all sharks, because of their sharp teeth and **aggressive** feeding habits, must be considered **potentially** dangerous. There is no relationship between the size of a shark and the risk of attack.

Nurse shark

Appearance: gray on top, white underneath, very heavily built, and large-finned.
Length: around 13 feet (4 m). *Weight*: 640 pounds (290 kg).
Temperament and habits: aggressive, often found close inshore.
Distribution: around eastern Australia.

Even with protective clothing, SEALs are at risk from a variety of ocean animals, including sharks, venomous sea snakes, and jellyfish.

Hammerhead shark

Appearance: flat, hammerlike head, long body.

Length: up to 18 feet (5.4 m). *Weight:* 880 pounds (400 kg).

Temperament: can be aggressive.

Distribution: **tropical** and **subtropical** waters.

Tiger shark

Appearance: gray on top, white underneath with a very wide head and jaws.

Length: 12–13½ feet (3.6–3.4 m). *Weight:* 1,900 pounds (870 kg).

Temperament and habits: often found close inshore, can be dangerous.

Distribution: tropical and subtropical waters.

Mako shark

Appearance: bright blue on top and creamy white underneath. Brightly colored.

Length: six to nine feet (1.8–2.7 m). *Weight*: 1,115 pounds (500 kg).

Temperament and habits: can swim very quickly, and sometimes leaps from the water when agitated.

Distribution: warm **temperate** waters.

Great white shark

Appearance: gray on top, white underneath, thick body, conical snout, and black eyes.

Length: up to 18 feet (6 m). *Weight:* 7,500 pounds (3,400 kg).

Temperament: very aggressive.

Distribution: found in all the warm and temperate oceans of the world, but especially off southern Africa, east and west of North America, and southern Australia and New Zealand.

Cow shark

Appearance: sandy gray with dark spots.

Length: up to nine feet (2.7 m). *Weight:* 1,300 pounds (590 kg).

Temperament and habits: swims close to the surface, aggressive.

Distribution: tropical and subtropical waters.

Sand shark

Appearance: white underneath, gray on top with yellow spots, hence its name.

Length: up to nine feet (2.7 m). *Weight:* 340 pounds (155 kg).

Temperament and habits: aggressive when provoked.

Distribution: tropical and subtropical waters.

Snaggletooth

Appearance: golden brown or gray in color.

Length: six feet (1.8 m). *Weight:* 75 pounds (35 kg).

Temperament and habits: can be found in shallow waters, can be aggressive.

Distribution: tropical waters.

Silvertip shark

Appearance: charcoal-colored, white tips on fins.

Length: nine feet (2.7 m). *Weight:* 183 pounds (83 kg).

Temperament and habits: fast and bold, potentially dangerous. Plentiful around reefs and islands.

Distribution: tropical and subtropical waters.

Gray reef shark

Appearance: gray, tail edged with black.

Length: six feet (1.8 m). *Weight:* 75 pounds (34 kg).

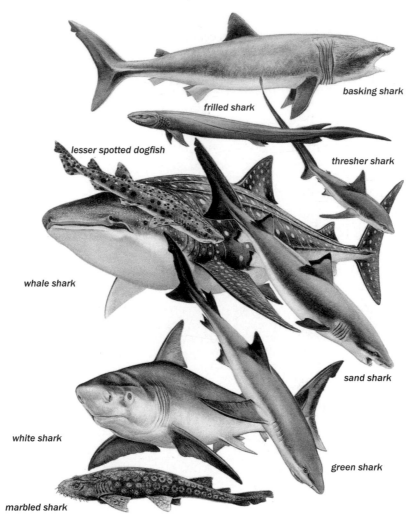

basking shark

frilled shark

lesser spotted dogfish

thresher shark

whale shark

sand shark

white shark

green shark

marbled shark

These are the some of the main shark species. Remember, the biggest are not necessarily the most dangerous. Some of the small ones, such as the sand shark, are easily provoked to attack.

Temperament and habits: curious, and aggressive when provoked.

Distribution: tropical waters.

Copper shark

Appearance: golden brown on top and cream underneath.

Length: 10 feet (3 m). *Weight:* 500 pounds (227 kg).

Temperament and habits: can be very aggressive.

Distribution: tropical and subtropical waters.

Bull shark

Appearance: gray on top, off-white underneath.

Length: 11½ feet (3.5 m). *Weight:* 670 pounds (305 kg).

Temperament and habits: dangerous—this is the most feared of tropical sharks.

Distribution: the tropics; will swim up rivers.

Blue shark

Appearance: brilliant blue on top, white underneath.

Length: 13 feet (4 m). *Weight:* 440 pounds (200 kg).

Temperament and habits: one of the most dangerous sharks in the ocean; responsible for many human **fatalities** and injuries.

Distribution: world-wide in tropical and temperate waters.

Beware of all sharks and try to ensure that you do not draw their attention. Sharks can be found in every ocean and sea, and can sense movement as well as blood and other decaying matter, such as vomit. Remember that not all fish you see with fins are sharks. For example, dolphins and porpoises can resemble sharks, and are rarely a threat to humans.

   Here's the SEALs' advice for avoiding sharks: Treat seasickness as soon as possible to avoid putting vomit in the water. If you do need to get rid of vomit, throw it as far away as possible behind the raft, so that the current sweeps it away. Try to limit the amount of urine or excrement that goes into the water at any one time. If you are cut or have been bitten, stop the bleeding as soon as possible. If on a dinghy or raft, do not dangle your limbs under the water. Like most predators, sharks will normally attack an animal that is showing signs of weakness. So if you are attacked, shout, slap the water, kick, or rap or poke the shark with a stick. These actions may be enough to persuade it to turn elsewhere. If there are other people in the water, huddle together facing outward, and beat the water with strong regular strokes. The shark will sense the confidence of your movements. Let your **adrenaline** fuel your anger and not your fear.

Unfortunately, sharks are not the only problem in the sea. There are many types of poisonous sea creatures you need to avoid at all costs. If in doubt, never eat a fish you are not sure about. Fish poisons are tasteless, and no amount of cooking will make the fish safe.

Eating poisonous fish can result in death in the worst cases. As soon as any symptoms arise—numbness, itching, or sickness—get the person to vomit by giving them saltwater to drink. There are other fish that are dangerous to touch, either because they have venomous spines, such as stonefish, or because they have poisonous barbs in their tails, such as rays. The spines inject a venom that is excruciatingly painful. Keep your shoes or boots on at all times when you are walking through saltwater, and use a stick, not your hands, to explore sand, rocks, and holes.

The main types of dangerous sea creature that the SEALs can recognize are listed here.

Auger or tenebra shell

These are slightly narrower than cone shells, and although their poison is less powerful, it is still very dangerous.

Blue-ringed octopus

These are deadly poisonous. Grayish white with blue, ringlike marks, blue-ringed octopuses are native to the Australian barrier **reef**. The poison they secrete is so powerful that it can kill prey even without contact.

Cone shell

Widely distributed in the Pacific and Indian Oceans, cone shells are very poisonous. They store up poison in a **duct** which is several times longer than the fish itself and inject it through a needle.

Moray eels

Powerful predators, they rest during the day, becoming active at night. They are common in warm tropical waters and have a dangerous bite. Adults can grow to five feet (1.5 m).

Portuguese man-of-war

Common in tropical water, especially off the Florida coast, it drifts in surface water, catching unwary fish in its tentacles. The tentacles, which can be 40 feet (12 m) long, contain stinging cells that can be fatal to humans.

Puffer fish

There are hundreds of varieties of this tropical fish. The delicately mottled Japanese variety is poisonous when eaten.

Rabbitfish

Rabbitfish are quite similar to sharks in their body structure, with five gill slits. They live and feed on the bottom of the ocean. The spine of the dorsal fin is very poisonous.

Rockfish, scorpionfish, lionfish

Saltwater fishes characterized by massive bodies and large heads armored with spines that inject poison that is sometimes lethal.

Sea snakes

Sea snakes are deadly poisonous. They are unlikely to bite, but stay well clear of them.

Stingray

Found in warm, shallow waters, stingrays use their dorsal fin as a highly poisonous spike. They have flattened and very extended bodies in which the tail is reduced to a defensive whip. They live and feed in sandy and muddy areas on the ocean bed. Sometimes they ascend rivers and into fresh water.

Stonefish

Any of several small, spiny venomous scorpion fish common about coral reefs of the Indian and Pacific oceans. Their natural camouflage makes them resemble stones or rocks. They dig themselves into the sea bed, making them almost impossible to see. Their sting is very painful and can be fatal.

Tang or surgeonfish

Tropical water fish with brightly colored markings. Surgeonfish get their name because of the presence of sharp, flat spines located on either side of the tail base that can inflict sharp cuts like a surgeon's scalpel.

Toadfish

Toadfish live among the seaweed of rocky coasts of warm seas. They have poisonous spines on the dorsal fins and gill covers. They have broad heads, large mouths, and strong teeth which they use to give a powerful bite if touched.

Triggerfish

Poisonous. When threatened, they can lock themselves in between rocks with the aid of their fins and cannot be pulled out.

MAKE CONNECTIONS: DEALING WITH JELLYFISH STINGS

A jellyfish sting can be extremely painful, and in extreme cases can be fatal. Dealing with stings quickly is important. First, get the victim out of the water as soon as possible because jellyfish stings may result in life-threatening convulsions. Remove tentacles or other bits of the jellyfish from the skin immediately, using clothing, seaweed, or other material. Do not rub the wound with anything, especially sand, because this may worsen the sting. Do not suck the wound. Do not urinate on the wound; it does not help. Try to deactivate the stingers by generously rinsing the affected area with vinegar for at least thirty seconds.

Tuna

Potentially dangerous. The most common tuna is the bluefin tuna which can grow to 15 feet (4.5 m) in length and attain a weight of 1,800 pounds (800 kg).

In general, SEALs are careful of fish that inhabit lagoons and reefs, and in particular of fish with small, parrotlike mouths and small belly fins. Yet the most common type of dangerous sea creature is the jellyfish. There are many different kinds of jellyfish. The largest can be six feet (1.8 m) in diameter, with tentacles hanging down to a depth of up to 100 feet (30 m).

These tentacles contain stinging cells that can inflict serious injury on the survivor. One of the deadliest is the sea wasp, which can cause death in as little as 30 seconds, though around three hours is normal.

RESEARCH PROJECT

Pick one dangerous sea creature described in this chapter and find out more about it. Write a report about where it lives, what it eats, how big it is, and what makes it so dangerous. Print photographs from the Internet of this creature to illustrate your report.

Steer clear of all jellyfish, especially since their tentacles may trail a long way from their body. Following a storm in tropical areas where large numbers of jellyfish are present, you may be stung by pieces of floating tentacles that have been broken off the jellyfish during the storm. Jellyfish washed up on a shore may look dead, but many can still inflict painful injuries. In general, try to get out of the water when jellyfish are present.

Other types of stinging creature include marine snails and slugs. As a survivor, you may come into contact with these when you are crossing coral reefs and sandy shores. You should avoid them; they can inject poison by plunging a barb into your flesh. The sting made by a cone shell is a puncture-type wound. When you are stung, the area around the wound will turn blue, swell, become numb, sting, and

The world's largest octopus is the North Pacific octopus, which can grow up to 30 feet (9 m) long and can weigh 150 pounds (68 kg).

TEXT-DEPENDENT QUESTIONS

1. Which kind of shark is one of the most dangerous?
2. Why might vomiting (throwing up) at sea put you in danger from sharks?
3. What should you do if a shark attacks you?
4. What is the most common dangerous sea creature?
5. What is the world's largest octopus?

burn. The degree of pain varies from person to person, though in all victims the numbness and tingling sensation around the wound quickly spreads through the whole body. This can be followed in a matter of hours by complete paralysis and death.

All SEALs are taught to respect the wildlife of the sea. The general rule is, if you stay away from dangerous sea creatures, they will be more likely to stay away from you.

RAFTS AND SAILING

If you need to survive at sea, a good raft will improve your chances. The U.S. Navy SEALs use modern boats, but they can also build seagoing rafts from the most basic materials if necessary.

If you are the survivor of a boat or aircraft disaster, there's a good chance that you will have an inflatable raft. Getting into these rafts from the water can be tricky. If the raft is attached to you with a rope, pull the raft toward you. Then grab handles on each side of the raft and pull yourself in, while kicking with your legs in the water. Another way of boarding is to get one knee inside the raft and pull yourself forward into it. When you are in the raft, make sure it is fully inflated, then check for any leaks.

You must remember one thing when afloat in the ocean: your raft will be at the mercy of winds and currents. Sea currents travel at speeds of less than 5 miles per hour (8 km/h), so movement is very slow. In areas where warm and cold currents meet, there will often be storms, dense fog, high winds, and heavy seas. These will make movement difficult and dangerous. Winds and waves can aid raft travel. To take advantage of the wind, you will need a sail. If the raft does not have one, make one from a piece of material.

Waves can be both helpful and dangerous. The size of waves is dependent upon the strength of the wind. Waves will move a raft only a few inches (several centimeters) at a time under normal conditions, so you will not move fast.

SEALs are adept at using standard issue Navy life rafts, but in an emergency, they must be able to construct one from found objects.

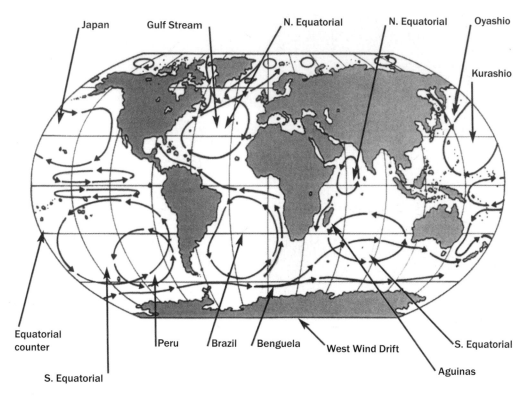

Currents are affected by wind, the ocean's salinity, and heat. Knowing how currents work can help you navigate if you are lost at sea.

Waves are useful indicators if you are searching for shallow areas or land. Ocean waves break when they enter shallow water or when they run into something. Use breaking waves as an aid to making a landfall. Waves can also capsize a raft in bad weather, or fill it with water.

All SEALs know how to make rafts if professional boats are not available. Rafts are better for river travel, but they can also be used for short sea journeys, such as traveling between islands in the tropics. Some small rafts, such as the brush raft, can be constructed very easily, though they are not recommended for lengthy travel. Rafts will not capsize easily if they are made properly, but you must remember the following points before setting out on your journey:

• Test your raft soundly in safe water before setting out.

MAKE CONNECTIONS: RIGHTING A CAPSIZED DINGHY

A capsized dinghy need not be a catastrophe in a survival situation at sea; you can right it easily if you know how.

- Grab the righting line from the opposite side.

- Brace your feet against the dinghy and pull.

- The dinghy should rise up and over, and will pull you temporarily out of the water.

- This procedure requires more effort in heavy seas or high winds.

- Tie all equipment securely to the raft or to the safety line. All survivors should have a rope tied around their waists and be secured to the raft.

The simplest raft for one person is the log flotation raft, for which you need two logs of light wood. Place the logs side by side about two feet (60 cm) apart and tie them together securely. You will then be able to float on them. Another easy raft to build is a vegetation raft. This is made out of small vegetation that will float. Place the plants in material or clothing to form a raft for equipment or people. (It will not hold heavy weights, though.)

If you have rope available, you can construct a simple log raft. Tie the logs securely together using the rope. Place two or more logs underneath running at right angles to the logs above. This gives your raft strength. Remember to cut notches into the logs and make sure the ropes run along them. These notches will stop the ropes from slipping over the logs once you are out at sea.

Landing a raft can be one of the most dangerous moments. If the land is likely

RESEARCH PROJECT

Stories about shipwrecks, desert islands, and survival at sea have always fascinated people, and many fiction books have been written about them over the years. Here are a few:

The Cave and the Sea by **John A. Heatherly**

Robinson Crusoe by **Daniel Defoe**

Life of Pi by **Yann Martel**

Swiss Family Robinson by **Johann David Wyss**

Your library should have at least one of these books. Read one and do a book report on it. Describe the events that happen to the characters. How true to life do you think the book is? Do the characters face any of the dangers described in the book you are reading now? Do they use any of the same skills used by the SEALs?

to have people living there, send a signal and wait for rescuers to come out to you. If you have to make a landing, choose your position carefully. Keep clear of rocks or strong surf. Look for gaps in the surf line. Go to the sheltered side of the island, where you will be protected from the wind. Strong tides may wash you back out to sea, so try to spot a sloping beach where the surf is less strong.

You may be carried along parallel to the beach and some distance out to sea by a rip current, or riptide. This is a surge of seawater escaping from the beach. Do not try to swim or paddle directly against the current. Swim or paddle along

The contents of a four-person life raft: sea anchor (A), paddles (B), first-aid kit (C), fishing line and hooks (D), bellow (E), quoit and line (F), survival leaflets (G), bailer (H), repair kit, flares, sponge, knife (I), water, can opener, cup, seasickness pills (J), flashlight and batteries (K), and resealing lids (L).

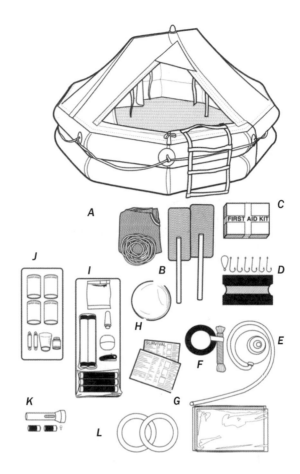

with the rip current for a short distance to allow its force to dissipate. Then head back in toward the shore. Beware of coral reefs in the Pacific—they will be difficult to see from low down in the water. Keep looking out for gaps.

Even if you have a good raft, it does not mean that you are safe. Living at sea can make you ill, so it is important that you know a few essential first-aid techniques used by the SEALs.

TEXT-DEPENDENT QUESTIONS

1. Describe two kinds of raft you might build if you were stranded at sea.
2. What should you do if you are caught in a rip current?

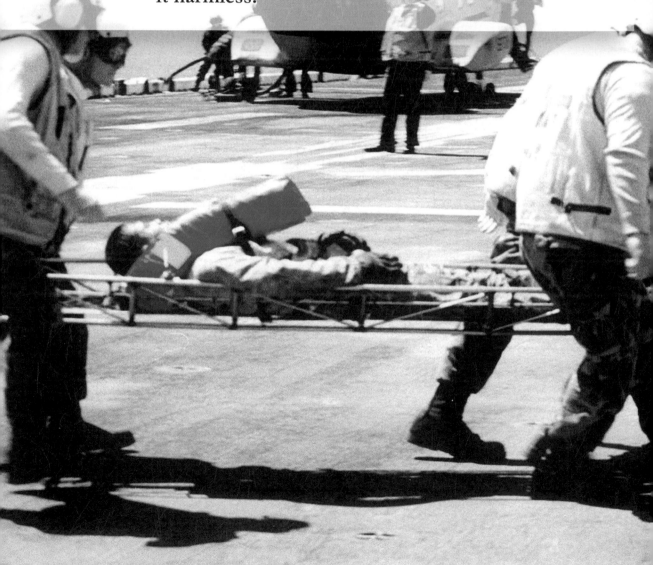

WORDS TO UNDERSTAND

intensifies: Makes stronger.

wary: Cautious, careful.

neutralize: Remove the danger from something, make
it harmless.

FIRST AID

Out in the ocean, there are few doctors on call. That is why the SEALs are experts in delivering survival first aid. Prompt attention to injuries and illnesses is needed to stop simple problems from becoming life threatening.

Even for tough SEALs, the greatest danger when you are surviving at sea is exposure to the elements. In a raft, do not expose yourself to the sun and wind needlessly. A SEAL will keep a layer of clothing on at all times, especially on the head. If you are very hot, dip your clothing in the sea, then wring it out and put it back on. Place any injured persons on the floor of the raft and make them comfortable. Try to keep them as warm or cool (depending on where you are), and as dry as possible.

Wear sunglasses or eye shields to protect your eyes from the glare of the sun. Be particularly careful about reflection off the water, which **intensifies** the sun's rays. Do not rub sore eyes; apply an antiseptic cream (if you have it) to the eye lids and bandage them lightly instead.

For parched lips and cracked skin, apply sunblock or Vaseline and do not lick your lips. Cover dry skin to prevent it becoming even dryer. Try to keep your clothing as dry as possible. Clean any sore that develops with fresh water and apply antiseptic cream. Large sores should be covered with a bandage, but change the bandages regularly.

An injured SEAL is carried aboard the amphibious assault ship, *U.S.S. Wasp*, after being saved by a search and rescue team.

Sunburns are very common problem in sea survival. Make sure that vulnerable skin is well covered. A sunburn can become a serious problem because it can lead to badly blistered, painful, and infected skin. As with all burns, do not burst any blisters. The best treatment is to use cold compresses (water-soaked material applied to the wound and re-soaked regularly to keep it chilled) for around 10 minutes. Also provide the victim with cold water to drink. Most importantly, get the victim into shelter—make one if need be.

Sometimes blisters can disable a large area of flesh. On the whole, do not burst them, because blisters form to help skin heal and keep out infection. However, there can be exceptions. If the blister stops the victim from moving easily, then you might have to break it. In this case bursting can be done through the following technique:

- Clean the area around the blister thoroughly using fresh water and soap if you have it. (Never use drinking water if you haven't got enough to spare.)

MAKE CONNECTIONS:
RESCUING A DROWNING PERSON

A drowning person usually goes into a blind panic, so unless the victim is in shallow water or you have been trained in water rescue techniques, do not be tempted to go in after them. It is better that you stay on the bank and throw them a buoyancy aid or a length of rope with which to pull them in. If you are forced to enter the water, take a buoyancy aid with you and give it to the victim upon reaching them. Try to calm the victim as much as possible.

Diving descent is always risky, because the increased water pressure can cause a dangerous vacuum to build up inside the mask or suit.

- Use a sterilized needle or blade to pierce the blister. Sterilization can be achieved by immersing the steel in alcohol, boiling it for about five minutes, or holding it over a flame. Even better would be to have sterilized needles sealed away in a medical pack.

- Pierce the blister at one end and let the fluid drain out. Do not pull away the blistered skin. Instead, let it stay there to protect the wound from infection.

- Cover the wound and clean it regularly. Keep checking to see if it is infected and apply some antibiotic ointment if you have it.

We have already seen that the sea is home to many of the world's most poisonous creatures. Knowing how to treat the injuries that these can give is an important part of SEAL training. Poisonous sea creatures deliver their venom in a variety of ways. Mostly they do it using poisonous spines, such as are found on stingrays and sea urchins. Or the poison is delivered by something called nematocysts. These are the stinging parts of creatures like jellyfish and anemones. They inject lots of tiny stinging cells, which stick themselves into the skin.

RESEARCH PROJECT

This book is based on the survival-at-sea techniques of the SEALs. Find out more about this elite military group. Which earlier U.S. military organizations did the SEALs grow from? During which war were the SEALs first started? What other wars and military conflicts have they been involved in? What role did they play in the death of Osama bin Laden? Describe SEAL training.

To treat spine poison, clean the wound with water, but be **wary** of any stinging bits stuck to the skin. Take these out carefully with tweezers. Treat this type of wound with heat. Place the wounded area in hot water, as hot as the victim can bear, for up to 90 minutes. The pain should slowly go away.

Nematocyst toxin is different because the poison stays on the skin to keep stinging. It should be washed off with large amounts of saltwater (not fresh water, which will only worsen stinging). Once this is done, scrape the sting site downward with a solid, flat object such as the back of a knife. If you can, soak the wound with vinegar for about 30 minutes to **neutralize** the stings. Following this, coat the wound in a powder (such as talcum), before brushing the talcum powder off, taking with it the remaining nematocysts. This is how the SEALs might deal with poisonous injuries.

One final injury deserves a mention for the sea survivor—how to get fish-hooks out of the skin. This is difficult because the hooks are designed to stay embedded. If you have to remove one, cut it away from the line and, if you

TEXT-DEPENDENT QUESTIONS
1. What is the best treatment for sunburn?
2. What are nematocysts?
3. Explain how to remove a fishhook from someone's skin.

have wire cutters, cut the barb (the sharp pronged piece at the end) as well. Once the barb is removed, hold the eye of the hook and take it back following the shape of the hook. If you don't have wire cutters, or the barb is embedded in the skin, then you have to push the barb forward and through the skin. Take hold of it with a cloth or other protective material, and withdraw it with the eye coming through last. This can be a painful procedure for the victim, so do it with a decisive, steady action until it is completed. Then dress the wound with a bandage.

Most problems at sea can be avoided by being careful in the first place. As we have seen, even though they are tough soldiers, the U.S. Navy SEALs still have a lot of respect for the sea. By treating the sea with caution and care, disasters are much less likely to happen and they will not have to use their survival skills.

SERIES GLOSSARY OF KEY TERMS

camouflage: Something that makes it hard to distinguish someone or something from the terrain or landscape around them.

casualty: A person who is killed or injured in a war or accident.

covert: Done in secret.

dehydrated: When you don't have enough water in your body for it to function properly. Alternatively, dehydrated food is food that has had all the water removed so that it won't go bad.

dislocation: When a joint is separated; when a bone comes out of its socket.

edible: Able to be eaten.

exposure: A health condition that results from bad weather around you. For example, when you get hypothermia or frostbite from cold weather, these are the results of exposure.

flares: A device that burns brightly, and can be used to signal for help. They can only be used once.

hygiene: The techniques and practices involved with keeping yourself clean and healthy.

improvised: Used whatever was available to make or create something. When you don't have professionally made equipment, you can make improvised equipment from the materials naturally found around you.

insulation: Something that keeps you warm and protects you from the cold.

kit: All of the clothing and equipment carried by a soldier.

layering: A technique of dressing for the wilderness that involves wearing many layers of clothing. If you become too warm or too cold, it is easy to remove or add a layer.

marine: Having to do with the ocean.

morale: Confidence, enthusiasm, and discipline at any given time. When morale is high, you are emotionally prepared to do something difficult. When morale is low, you might be angry, scared, or anxious.

purification: The process of making water clean and safe enough to drink.

terrain: The physical features of a stretch of land. Hard or rough terrain might be mountains or thick forests, and easy terrain would be an open field.

windbreak: Something that you use to block the wind from hitting you. If you camp somewhere exposed to the wind, it will be very difficult to stay warm.

FURTHER READING

Bahmanyar, Mir and Chris Osman. *SEALs: The US Navy's Elite Fighting Force*. Oxford, England: Osprey Publishing, 2011.

Butler, William. *66 Days Adrift: A True Story of Disaster and Survival on the Open Sea*. Camden, Me.: International Marine, 2005.

Colwell, Keith. *Sea Survival Handbook: The Complete Guide to Survival at Sea*. New York: Skyhorse Publishing, 2009.

Mann, Don and Ralph Pezzullo. *The U.S. Navy SEAL Survival Handbook: Learn the Survival Techniques and Strategies of America's Elite Warriors*. New York: Skyhorse Publishing, 2012.

U.S. Navy. *The U.S. Navy SEAL Guide to Fitness and Nutrition*. New York: Skyhorse Publishing, 2007.

Ward, Nick. *Left for Dead: Surviving the Deadliest Storm in Modern Sailing History*. New York: Bloomsbury USA, 2007.

ABOUT THE AUTHOR

Dr Chris McNab has written and edited numerous books on military history and elite forces survival. His publications to date include *German Paratroopers of World War II, The Illustrated History of the Vietnam War, First Aid Survival Manual*, and *Special Forces Endurance Techniques*, as well as many articles and features in other works. Forthcoming publications include books on the SAS, while Chris's wider research interests lie in literature and ancient history. Chris lives in South Wales, U.K.

INDEX